God is <u>NEVER</u> on Vacation!
One Man's Mission to Feed the Homeless

David Timothy
a.k.a. SoupMan

© 2008-2009 David Timothy, Dallas, TX

All rights reserved. Copyright includes but is not limited to printed books, electronic media, and email transmissions.

Registered trademarks, trademarks, service marks, and copyrights in this book are the property of their respective owners.

Excerpts and quotes from this book may be used by individuals without permission from the author.

For permission to use excerpts or quotations in commercial work, email David Timothy at david@soupmobile.org

ISBN 10 is 1517269962
ISBN 13 is 9781517269968
10 9 8 7 6 5 4 3 2 1

Dedication

To my dear friend Sheryl. You were the one who believed in me. You were the one who asked me that magical question, "What do you really want to do with your life?" When I answered, "I want to feed the homeless," you were the one who said, "I know you can do it!" You were the one who cheered me on every step of the way. You were the one who pointed your finger at me and said, "Then you will be the SoupMan."

You were the one that somehow knew this little Bumble Bee could actually fly.

Sheryl, it's with grateful appreciation that I dedicate this book to you. Your kind and giving heart is a constant inspiration to me. I am blessed to know you. Thanks for believing!

Your friend always,
David Timothy, a.k.a. SoupMan.

Special Thanks

My grateful thanks to the wonderful women who edited this book: LeAnne Baird and Linda Graf.

Thank you for your patience, diligence, and attention to detail as you so carefully edited a book written from my heart.

I am most grateful to you both for the gift of your time and energy to help me. This book would not have been published without your efforts. Most importantly, thank you for your kind and generous friendship. It is my privilege to know you both. God bless you and yours.

Chapter 1
The Journey Begins

If you can't feed a hundred people, then feed just one.   Mother Teresa

As a young boy growing up in Detroit, Michigan, I dreamed about growing up to be a cowboy, an astronaut, a movie star, or maybe even the President of the United States. But I never dreamed I would grow up to become the SoupMan.

As a child, I often experienced hunger first-hand. And while I was never homeless, food was scarce and we often wondered where the next meal was coming from. It wasn't just hunger, there was the fear that went with it. The fear that the next meal would not be there. As an adult missing a meal is no big deal for me. That's because I know there will be food for the next meal. As a child there was no guarantee the next meal would be there.

Little did I know that the hunger I suffered as a child would influence my life's path over a half century later.

Now as an adult (and as the SoupMan) I am surrounded by lots of food. The SoupMobile warehouse is loaded with tons of food that comes in and goes out every week. We have army of volunteers, donors, supporters and prayer warriors who share my dream of feeding the homeless.

I wasn't always the SoupMan. Officially I didn't become the SoupMan until 2003 when I started the SoupMobile. Unofficially the real beginnings of the SoupMan started in 1989. That was the year I married a beautiful young lady by the name of......

Chapter 2

Peggy's Story

It was the best of times . . .
— Charles Dickens, A Tale of Two Cities

In 1989 Peggy and I were married. Little did I know at the time that God was beginning my training as the SoupMan.

Peggy was a former cheerleader with lots of energy and plenty of pizzazz. She could light up a room with her amazing upbeat personality. She had a heart of gold and a real caring for her fellow man. I considered myself lucky to be marrying her. We looked forward to a life of love, fun and prosperity.

However fate seemed to have a far different plan for us. I remember the day we said our "I do's." We were both at the peak of our games. We were in great health and doing fairly well in our business lives. We had lots of friends and were enjoying the good life. Everything looked to be coming up roses. How quickly it all came to an end. Literally within days of getting married Peggy started having some health issues. She was having trouble with her balance and felt fatigued.

So off to the Doctor we headed. We weren't too concerned. After all she was a former cheerleader who was now a fitness buff. She exercised every day, lifted weights and was fanatical about eating properly. The Doctor checked her out and said she was simply overworked and needed to take it easy for a while. So no worries. Our life together would still come up roses. But there was one small problem. The Doctor was wrong. It wasn't overwork; it wasn't stress; it wasn't some minor health problem. It was...

---MULTIPLE SCLEROSIS—

Chapter 3

The Journey Gets Rough

I know God will not give me anything I can't handle. I just wish that He didn't trust me so much.
Mother Teresa

We still weren't too worried. We didn't know much about M.S., but we felt confident that the Doctor could write her a prescription and that would take care of it. How naive we were! To our dismay, we learned that not only was there was no cure for MS, but the best the doctors could do was prescribe medication to *maybe* delay the progression of the disease. Suddenly her life, and mine, wasn't coming up roses anymore.

I remember remaining cool and collected in Peggy's presence, but the first chance I could be alone I screamed out at God. I howled at how unfair this was. I ranted that this just wasn't right. I told him that when we said our vows this wasn't what we had signed up for. Oh sure, we said "in sickness and in health," but we didn't really think the sickness part applied to us. After all, we had been at the peak of our game.

God didn't seem to be listening to me. So I continued to rail against him, and called him every name in the book and some that weren't in the book. I was a madman. I accused God over and over again of being on vacation. Looking back it wasn't my proudest moment.

So began a journey that lasted 15 long, difficult, and sometimes brutal years. No way was I going to accept the doctors' verdict that there was no cure for MS. Not me, not Mr. Successful, not Mr. Peak of My Special Universe.

When I was alone, I continued my tirade with God, but I never let on that anything was amiss, for Peggy's sake. For the next 15 years I remained a tower of strength. On the outside I remained composed and seemed to be an external optimist. On the inside, I constantly accused God of being on vacation. His silence was maddening. I felt like he had abandoned us. Well with or without him, I was determined to forge ahead.

If we had to travel to the end of the earth to find a cure, that's what we'd do. What we ended up doing was not too far removed from that very thing. Within a short time of Peggy's MS diagnosis, I resigned from my day to day business activities.

We agreed that we would leave Michigan to seek a cure that we would end up chasing for the next 15 years.

We sold all of our stuff, said goodbye to our friends, packed the car, and started driving.

We first headed south because the doctors told us she would do better in a milder climate. When we got to the South, we traded in our car and bought a Recreational Vehicle. Many people wait until they retire, buy an RV, and travel the country in style. We bought our RV so we could travel from place to place to find a cure for Peggy's illness.

For the next decade-and-a-half we crisscrossed the country traveling to Florida, Washington, New Mexico, Arizona, back to Michigan, Tennessee, Texas and many other states in between.

Sometimes we stayed in one place for months, sometimes for years. We had become nomads in search of the ultimate prize—a cure for Peggy.

How long we stayed at any one location depended on how successful the treatments were. We tried everything from conventional medicine to holistic medicine, from special diets to acupuncture. Nothing seemed to work. No dice.

For 15 years I had a ringside seat as I watched her slowly decline from the vibrant former cheerleader I had married to a struggling, bedridden invalid.

I quickly went from being a husband to being a full time caregiver. Yes, a husband in name, but for all practical purposes I had become a full time nurse. As a little boy growing up in Detroit, nurse/caregiver wasn't one of the professions I had dreamed of becoming as an adult. I didn't waste a lot of time feeling sorry for myself. I was too busy feeling sorry for Peggy. She was the one who really suffered. Going from a totally dynamic and independent woman to needing to be fed and bathed was not an easy thing.

I learned by experience that being a caregiver is one of the most difficult jobs on earth. On duty 24/7. Never a chance to be completely alone with myself. Always on watch. Over the years I had several doctors advise me to put her into a nursing home. Sometimes I considered that alternative, but I discarded it. I could not imagine letting strangers caring for her most basic needs, and I wanted her to be able to retain as much dignity as possible. I know she would have done the same for me had the situation had been reversed.

Chapter 4

A Cruel Twist of Fate

Ever has it been that love knows not its own depth until the hour of separation.
>   Kahlil Gibran

Then my life with Peggy suddenly came to an abrupt end. Fifteen years into the marriage and after 15 years of watching her slowly slip away, she died in her sleep on her 48th birthday. It was completely unexpected. While she did struggle with MS and was virtually bedridden, the Doctors didn't feel like she was in any immediate danger. They confidentially told me she could certainly live at least another ten years, and if there were breakthroughs in medical science, probably longer.

So when she passed away in her sleep we were all stunned.

The week before her 48th birthday, I bought her several birthday presents. I got her a stuffed bear and some tapes of the old Andy Griffith TV show. By then she didn't have much joy in her life, but she loved to watch Andy Griffith reruns. We would watch the reruns together and it was one of the increasingly rare times I heard her laugh. The sad fact was that she was at a point in her life she just didn't have much to laugh about.

I carefully wrapped the gifts the night before her birthday and set them alongside her birthday cake. I even put 29 candles on the cake to make her laugh. But sometime in the early morning hours of her 48th birthday she quietly passed away in her sleep. So quietly that I was not even aware of it. This in itself was pretty amazing.

As any caregiver knows, you become super sensitive to your patient. After 15 years I had got to the point where I could be in the other room and if Peggy just breathed a little differently I would know it.

Sometimes I would not even hear anything, but I could sense something wasn't quite right and I would rush to her aid. I know this may sound farfetched to some of you, but I assure you it's absolutely true. Ask any mother. They are incredibly sensitive and alert to the needs of their child. That's how I had become with Peggy. I still wonder how she slipped away without me knowing it. For a long time after her death I felt guilty about this. What happened to my super sensitivity the night she died. How could I have been so lax. How could I have not noticed and awoken and saved her. I felt like a complete failure. Fifteen years of faithful watching and then one night where it seemed like I was off duty. It took me a while to get over my guilt and come to the realization that there was nothing I could have done. Now I am at peace with it, but at the time my guilt was overwhelming. I had failed. In fifteen years I had gone from Mr. Successful, Mr. Peak of My Game to a total and complete failure.

Here is all it all went down......

Chapter 5

Losing Peggy

. . . it was the worst of times.
— Charles Dickens, A Tale of Two Cities

The morning of Peggy's 48th birthday I got out of bed, lightly tapped her on the shoulder and said, "Happy Birthday, beautiful." There was no response. I said it a little louder and there was still no response. At first I thought she was just joking around, and said, "hey birthday girl, time to get up and open your presents." Still no response. All of a sudden a sense of doom came over me—something wasn't right.

I gave her a firm shake. Nothing. I loudly called her name. Nothing. I checked her pulse. Nothing. All of a sudden I became a madman again, just like 15 years ago when we learned that she had M.S.

I grabbed the phone and called 911, shouting at the operator to send some help. It seemed like hours until help arrived but in less than two minutes I heard the sirens streaking toward us. It happens that the fire station was just down the street.

The paramedic rushed into the house and I directed him into the bedroom. He asked me to leave the room. I screamed "NO WAY." He turned her over, checked her pulse and looked at her ashen face, then said to me, "She's gone." I grabbed him by the shoulders and shouted, "**GET HER BACK!**"

He said "sir I'll try, but I need you to leave the room so I can work." A police officer who had just arrived took me outside. Looking back, I now know the paramedic knew he could not revive her, but he needed to get me out of the room to calm me down. I wasn't willing to let her go without a fight. I had cared for her for 15 years and I was determined to do it for another 15 years. While the police officer outside tried to calm me down, the neighbors slowly gathered around.

Then other paramedics took a stretcher into our home. Minutes later they brought her out on the stretcher and the original paramedic had some kind of breathing apparatus on her face. He was frantically pumping it as they were all rushing to the ambulance.

Hope flickered in me that she would be alright. Everything seemed to be moving in slow motion but I know now they were moving very quickly.

Right at that moment one of my neighbors pulled up in her car and said to get in, and she would take me to the hospital. The hospital was only about 10 minutes away but it was the longest 10 minutes of my life.

When we got to the hospital I leapt out of the car and ran into the emergency room. I cut in front of everyone and ran right up to the nurses' desk and shouted, "how is she doing." Of course they had no idea who I was talking about. I said, "I'm Peggy's husband". Of course still not enough information for them. I screamed, "don't you know who I am?" I didn't say that to infer that I was anyone important, just that I was the husband of the woman they had just brought in. The kind woman at the front desk quickly realized she was dealing with a madman. She said "just show me your driver's license and I will handle everything."

Meanwhile, my lady neighbor was at my side urging me to take a seat while they checked on Peggy's status. I finally sat down and waited in stunned silence, feeling the eyes of the other people in the waiting room looking at me as if I were a madman. I was! I didn't care, all I wanted to hear was that Peggy would be okay. After a while one of the nurses came out and asked me to come into the back.

Waiting there for me was one of the doctors. He started talking some medical stuff and I cut him off and said, "how's she doing." He slowly dipped his head and with a look of sorrow said, "she's expired." I had never heard that term before, but I knew exactly what he meant. She was gone forever. I didn't say a word. I just leaned against the wall and slid down to the floor and sobbed uncontrollably.

During the entire 15 years of Peggy's illness I had never cried—not one tear, not one single tear. I felt that I had to be strong for her. But now the floodgates opened and the tears flowed like they never before in my life. After that everything was in a fog. That same kind neighbor took me home.

I sat alone, stunned, on the couch at home. Thelma, our 8 lb. Chihuahua, jumped on my lap. She was shaking. She knew something was very wrong. I held her like there was no tomorrow.

Thelma had always been a fiercely loyal to Peggy. Whenever a traveling nurse or a neighbor would enter our home to visit with Peggy, Thelma would leap between them and Peggy and starting barking in her most ferocious manner. I would always have to hold Thelma to calm her down. As I sat holding her in my arms on the couch I looked around the room and spotted Peggy's gifts and birthday cake. I was overwhelmed with sadness. She hadn't even had a chance to open her gifts and eat her cake. There would be no birthday celebration that day.

Chapter 6

Life Without Peggy

The joy of our heart is ceased, our dance is turned into mourning.
Lamentations 5: 15

Looking back, I suspect Peggy did not pass away on her 48th birthday by accident. I think that late the night before, in the early morning hours of her birthday, she decided she had enough.

No more birthdays where I actually had to open her gifts for her because her hands were not nimble enough. No more birthdays where I would have to blow the candles out for her because she did not have enough breath. No more birthdays where I had to spoon-feed her cake. No more birthdays where she was bedridden.

I think she just said "no more." Peggy was a strong Christian and a firm believer. I think she had enough of her brutal life, and yearned to be in the gentle arms of Jesus. Later that week I opened her birthday gifts and gently put them in her casket to be buried with her. I like to think that somewhere up there in heaven she is holding her stuffed bear and watching the Andy Griffith videos. Earth's loss is heaven's gain.

For months after the funeral I was dazed and disoriented. I had trouble doing the simplest things.

When I would go grocery shopping I would start putting stuff in the grocery cart that Peggy had previously eaten as part of her special medical diet. I would get to the check out and realize that most of the stuff in the cart was for her. But of course she wasn't here any more. In the last years of her life she had come to really like chicken soft tacos from Taco Bell. They weren't part of her diet, but on occasion as a special treat I would stop by the Taco Bell drive thru and get her some. I never liked them much myself, but she thought they were just great.

About a month after she died, I found myself in the drive thru of Taco bell. Out of the speaker I heard a voice say, "may I help you." I just sat there in stunned silence. There was nothing I wanted. I was stopping to get something for Peggy. The voice said again, "may I help you." I couldn't speak. I could barely breathe. I just sadly put the car in gear and drove off.

Then about three months after Peggy's death, I ran into that original paramedic that had been first on the scene when I had called 911. I spotted him when I was driving to work. He was on standby at the scene of a car accident. Thankfully, no one had been seriously injured.

I pulled my car over and got out and introduced myself and asked, "do you remember me?" You came to my home three months ago to try to save my wife. He did remember me and said he was very sorry for my loss. I said no, "I'm the one who is very sorry." I'm sorry for screaming and yelling at you as you tried to do your job. I told him I had been out of my mind and knew I had acted like a madman. He kindly nodded his head and said he completely understood. I apologized again and thanked him for getting there so fast and doing the best he could for Peggy.

I shook his hand and left there with a new appreciation for all of our first-line defenders. Police, firefighters, paramedics, nurses, doctors, and of course, caregivers.

Chapter 7

God Always Has a Plan!

When God puts a burden upon you,
He puts His own arms underneath.
Charles Sturgeon

When Peggy had first become sick I felt like God had gone on vacation and had abandoned us. I was wrong.

Now I know he was there all the time. What I didn't know was his plan for me when the 15 years started. He hadn't bothered to tell me in advance. It's a good thing he didn't, because I guarantee you that if I knew in advance what he was planning I would have said, NO WAY!

Earlier in this book I said that even though I didn't officially become the SoupMan until 2003—the year I started the SoupMobile, the beginning of unofficially becoming the SoupMan actually started in 1989. That was the year that Peggy and I got married and then there was that 15 long years until her death.

Little did I know that during that 15 years God was training me to be the SoupMan. He was preparing me for my life's work which is to feed and care for the homeless. He was molding me to be a man of caring, love and compassion. One man started that 15 year odyssey and a different one emerged.

It's not that I was a bad guy when the 15 years started. I wasn't a bank robber, I hadn't killed anyone, and I wasn't that hard to get along with. I think most people would have said I was a pretty decent guy. I would always put money in the Salvation Army kettle at Christmas and once in a rare while I would even volunteer somewhere. I thought I was a pretty cool dude.

I told you earlier that when Peggy and I married I was at the peak of my game. Successful, well liked, a man about town, lots of friends, and the envy of most men because I was marring this beautiful vibrant former cheerleader. Yes, I thought I had 'arrived.'

In truth I was selfish. I was pretty much only into me. **MY** needs, **MY** friends, **MY** successful business, the peak of **MY** game. It was all about **me.**

It wasn't that I mistreated others or gave people a bad time. It was just that I was the focus of my life on this planet. Devoting my life to feeding and caring for the homeless. Ha, not a chance. Up until my marriage to Peggy I devoted my life to feeding and caring for **me.**

So it seems God stepped in and said, I am NOT well pleased with this guy who seems to be pretty pleased with himself. I'm going to have to give him a course correction and mold him into the kind of guy I will be pleased with. Let me tell you, when God decides to start molding you, things can get pretty intense. He doesn't mess around. Yes, that 15 years was brutal for Peggy, but it wasn't a cake walk for me either.

My life as Mr. Successful, Mr. Peak of My Game came to a screeching halt. In place of it was the life of a caregiver. It was a totally humbling experience for me. I went from Mr. Man about town being served at the finest restaurants, to the one who was doing the serving.

God had put up a stop sign in my selfish life style and said, "No more---now it's time to put someone else first in your life." That's what a care giver has to do. Now I have a totally new respect for caregivers. Especially family members who are caregivers. They don't get paid for their work, they are on duty 24/7, they live and die on every turn of health of the patient, and literally put their own life on hold. That's what I ended up doing for 15 years. I didn't sign up for it, I didn't want it, I didn't like it, but it was just what I needed to become the SoupMan. It seems God knew what he was doing all along.

Now here's where things get even more remarkable. As the SoupMan I have become a caregiver all over again. But this time as a caregiver for the homeless, it's different. I did sign up for it, I do want it, I do like it and I guarantee you that I get far more out of it that I put into it. My life is far more satisfying as a giver than as a taker. The joys of giving go far beyond what anyone could imagine.

Before the 15 year odyssey began I thought I needed a lot of stuff. A fancy place to live, fancy cars, fancy restaurants, and of course all about me. Now I'm perfectly content in my small 1000 square foot home with its tiny backyard, totally satisfied with my 2002 Chrysler PT Cruiser, remarkably happy sharing my tuna sandwich with a homeless person while sitting under a bridge, and in total peace knowing it's not all about me. It took God 15 years to make those changes in my very being. That in itself is a little embarrassing. I was so far gone the wrong way it took him 15 years to turn me around.

By the way, as the SoupMan I don't think that I'm anything special or better than anyone else. For me there is only that special 'ONE'. So even though my life is remarkably different now from when that 15 years began, I have no illusions that I have 'arrived.' In fact I know I have not! Now for me it's about three magic words......

Chapter 8

Feed My Sheep

At the end of life we will not be judged by how many diplomas we have received, how much money we have made, how many great things we have done. We will be judged by 'I was hungry, and you gave me something to eat, I was naked and you clothed me. I was homeless, and you took me in.'

Mother Teresa

Jesus said "Feed My Sheep." In those three words, I believe he was referring to far more than just passing out food, or once in a while showing that you care by doing a good deed. Jesus also spoke about bringing spiritual shelter, love, caring, and most of all, hope, to people who are in need. That's what the SoupMobile is about!

When I am taking volunteers in the SoupMobile van to serve food to homeless people, I tell them we have two missions for the day. Our secondary mission is feeding the homeless. Our number one mission is to bring our love to the homeless. Yes, the food is souper-important, but love is what feeds their souls.

What's remarkable about all of this is that this kind of thinking just comes naturally to me now. But even more remarkable is that at one time in my life I could not even imagine this kind of thought. I was so into 'me' that I really couldn't be into anyone else. Oh sure, I knew the words about loving your neighbor like yourself. But putting those words into practice was not actually something that I was interested in doing. However my 15 year odyssey took care of that. Never in a million years would I have learned this on my own. God had to patiently teach me. No, he did not abandon me during that 15 years. He was not on vacation. He was teaching me!

Another important thing that God taught me during that 15 year odyssey was this. Remember earlier I said that when the 15 years started I wasn't a bad guy, hadn't killed anyone, I wasn't that hard to get along with and thought most people who have said I was a pretty decent guy.

I have learned that's not enough. It's not enough just to coast through life just remaining in neutral--- Not doing too much bad and mainly doing good that benefits *yourself*, not others. I am reminded of the following Bible verse.

James 4:17 Therefore, to him who knows to do good and does not do it, to him it is sin.

Those of us who have been blessed in this life are expected to reach out to the less fortunate. We are expected to use our talents, our time, our resources to reach out to the 'least of these.' No, it's not enough to just stay neutral. If we know to do good, we must then do it! The beauty of it all is that if you 'do it,' you will get far more out of it than you give. I am living proof of this.

Okay, so now I was wanting to Feed His Sheep. Nice sounding words, but just how does one go about doing that. It's one thing to say that you want to do something, but it's entirely a different thing to actually do it.

You already know about my own hunger as a child. That gave me a compassion for the homeless who struggle to find food every day. You also know about that 15 year odyssey that took me from 'it's all about me' to 'it's all about them.' What you don't know is about the birth of the SoupMobile in 2003. The ministry that God would have me use to 'Feed His Sheep'....

Chapter 9
The SoupMan, a.k.a. A Bumble Bee

Aerodynamically, the bumble bee shouldn't be able to fly, but the bumble bee doesn't know it so it goes on flying anyway.

Mary Kay Ash

So how did the SoupMobile get started in August of 2003? I had always remembered the hunger I experienced as a child. Added to that, the changes God had made in me during my 15 year odyssey. And I remembered the words in the Bible where Jesus said "Feed My Sheep." That combination of things got me thinking about feeding the homeless.

I had told no one of my dream of feeding the homeless. It was just a thought in my head. That thought started to gain traction when a very good friend of mine by the name of Sheryl asked me something in early 2003 that no one had ever asked me before. She asked me, "what do you really want to do with your life?"

I still get pretty excited when I think back to her asking me that question. For a moment I was totally silent. I could see she was serious and really wanted to hear what I had to say.

So I took a deep breath and said very quietly, **"I want to feed the homeless."** Only six words, but one's I had never spoken to a human being before. I will always remember Sheryl's response. "I know you can do it!" Well I was glad she knew I could do it, because I didn't have a clue how I would do it.

So began the journey from a thought in my head to the start of the SoupMobile. Now that the genie was out of the bottle and I had spoken those six magic words, **"I want to feed the homeless,"** I was on the journey of my life. I was about to find out for sure if God was on vacation or not!!!

The first question was how? How could I do this when I didn't have any resources whatsoever? I had no experience feeding the homeless. Absolutely none. I didn't have the financial resources to do it and I certainly did not have the backing to do it. Really all I had was a vision and Sheryl saying, "I know you can do it." So I started praying about it and drawing up different ways I could feed the homeless. First I considered a regular soup kitchen where the homeless would come to our location every day for a meal. That's what I had always seen on TV.

Every year when the holidays would roll around there would be some 'feel good' TV shows about holiday cheer and there would always be that scene in the soup kitchen where some grizzled old man was smiling as he was eating the hearty soup.

That was the only concept of a soup kitchen that I had ever known. As I considered that concept for my soup kitchen I knew there would be several major roadblocks. Not the least of these would be, what we in the business call NIMBY—not it my back yard. No one wants a soup kitchen in their neighborhood. They know it will attract the homeless and that's not always good for property values.

So I had to come up with Plan B. And like a bolt of lightening it came to me in a flash. If the homeless could not come to my place to eat, I would take the food to them. Yes, a MOBILE soup kitchen. I would load up my mobile soup kitchen with food and take it to the places where the homeless already congregate. It was pure genius. It was pure God. I'm not smart or wise enough to come up with that kind of idea on my own.

Once I had the concept down, then I started searching for a name for my soup kitchen. I considered names like, Food Van, Hunger Van, Food Van for the Homeless, Mobile food for the Homeless, and many more. None of them seemed right. Then like a bolt of lightening it came to me.

I would call it the SoupMobile. It was pure genius. It was pure God. Now I was getting somewhere. I had a concept and a name. I still had a long way to go, but it was with great excitement that I told all of this to Sheryl. I will never forget her response. She looked me straight in the eye, pointed her finger at me and said, "then you will be the SoupMan." At the time I chuckled and said, "you may be right."

Little did I know that her prophetic words would come true and then some. While my given name is David Timothy, I think more people know me as the SoupMan. In truth they are one in the same. I am the SoupMan 24/7. I live it, I breathe it, I am it. The SoupMan is my very being.

Sometimes if I am in a crowded room and someone calls out the name David, I don't even respond. It's not that I am being rude, I just think they are calling out for another David in the room. I'm so used to being called the SoupMan, sometimes I forget the David part.

By the way, I don't mean that I 'work' as the SoupMan 24/7. I've learned to take time out for myself. I've also learned to pace myself and I've learned to delegate. As the SoupMan I've become a caregiver for thousands and thousands of homeless men and women.

However it's important that you know that I am not a one man band. I am surrounded by an army of friends, volunteers, donors, supporters and prayer warriors who are the true heart and soul of the SoupMobile. The SoupMobile is not an **'I'** thing, it's a **'WE'** thing. But I'm getting ahead of myself.

So now I had a concept—a mobile soup kitchen, a name—the SoupMobile, and even a nickname—the SoupMan. Nothing else! No money, no donors, no deep pocket supporters, no sources of food, no mobile van, no umbrella church or organization to support us and most important no tax exempt status from the I.R.S. Blissfully I was like the Bumble Bee that doesn't know it can't fly. I didn't know that I couldn't start a major charity without major backing.

I know it now, but I didn't know it back then. So not knowing I couldn't do it, I started doing it.

My first step was a little unusual. I went out and bought some personalized license plates for my 2002 PT Cruiser, which by the way was mostly owned by the bank at that time. I have since paid it off and I am blissfully unaware that I need anything better.

Can you guess what the word was on those personalized plates? Sure you can! It was SoupMan. Putting those plates on my car was a total leap of faith. I mean like all I had to this point was a concept, a name and a nickname and here I was advertising to the world that I was the SoupMan. It didn't matter, I was committed and there was no going back. Most important, was that I didn't know that I couldn't do it. I was just a happy go lucky Bumble Bee.

Next up I decided I needed a van to deliver the food. After all the SoupMobile was a 'mobile' soup kitchen. So with very little money I started looking at used vans. All of them cost too much. I finally found a 1985 Ford Econoline Van with 250,000 miles on it.

The price was right and now we had wheels. I felt like a 16 year old kid who just got his first car. Since I already had a personalized SoupMan license plate for my car, I decided I needed one for the van. Of course our first van would also have to have a very special personalized license plate. Can you guess what I put on those van plates. Sure you can! It was Soup 1. In honor of our first feeding van and with expectations of more vans to come. Since that time we have added   Soup 2, a 2006 Chevy Van which was donated to us by a local banker who read about our old 85 van in an article in the Dallas Business Journal. As he was presenting me the keys to the van he said, "when I read the article about your old van and how many miles you had on it, I felt called by the Lord to get you a new one." And that's just what he did.

Since that time I have had some people tell me it's time to get rid of Soup 1 and take it to the scrap heap. I only have one word to say about that. NO WAY! Okay that's two words, but you get the point. Soup 1 runs rough, goes slow, is well worn around the edges, but it was the one who brung us to the dance.

Soup 1 will always be part of fleet. In fact my dream is to one day have an 'off the frame' restoration of Soup 1. For you non-car buffs, that means literally stripping the van down to its frame and completely rebuilding it to make it as good as new. Anyway that's my dream and with God as my pilot those dreams seems to have a way of coming true. Got vehicle restoration skills? Call the SoupMan.

So now I had the big three. A concept (mobile soup kitchen), a name (SoupMobile) and a van (Soup 1). Oh, and let's not forget my new nickname—The SoupMan. However I noticed that I was missing some key pieces that were needed to run a mobile soup kitchen. Things like no money, no help, no food, no donors, no volunteers and a mailing list that consisted of five people. Major problems one might think, but not for this Bumble Bee. Remember I didn't know I couldn't fly. So I started by contacting local food stores and asking for food donations. That was slow going at first, but eventually some food started coming in.

Everyone I met I told them about the SoupMobile and gently urged them to help in any way they could. Again slow going but eventually some help and small amounts of money started coming in. As for volunteers I had only one in the beginning. Today I am surrounded by an army of volunteers who are the true heart and soul of the SoupMobile. That original volunteer was a wonderful lady by the name of Cynthia. She was a home health care provider who helped me take care of Peggy in the last year of her life. Cynthia is an angel from heaven and has a heart of gold. She too was a Bumble Bee. She didn't know we couldn't fly either. Cynthia believed in the SoupMobile so much she was one of the original members of our Board of Directors and she still is to this day.

Chapter 10

Wagons Ho!

" Dream Big, Baby..."　　　　The SoupMan

It was time for the SoupMobile to make its first run. Time to fly. But now we had another problem. Where should we go with our mobile soup kitchen to feed the homeless.I really didn't know anything about the homeless or where they hung out. All I knew was they must need food.

Of course I didn't consider this obstacle a major problem. Remember I was a Bumble Bee. So I just started driving Soup 1 into downtown Dallas. Eventually I spotted a few guys that looked homeless. I stopped the van and asked them if they were hungry. They said yes and I fed them with some of the meager provisions we had. Then having filled their stomachs I asked them for help. I said, "hey, where do the homeless hang out around here?"

They told me that a lot of the homeless lived in cardboard box cities under the expressways. So with that information I started driving on the side streets that ran along the side of the expressways. Now Dallas is a big city and it took me a while to find the homeless I wanted to serve. Finally I struck pay dirt. There it was, a literal city of homeless people living under the overhead expressway. It looked like a subdivision of homes you might see in a suburban neighborhood. Except instead of wood and brick houses, there were hundreds of cardboard boxes lined up in rows. Those boxes were the homes the homeless were living in.

So I took a deep breath and drove Soup 1 right up into the box camp. I didn't have a clue of what I was doing or getting into. I got out of my van and just stood there for a few minutes. I was a stranger in their city and I didn't know how I would be received. Would they think I was friend or foe. Maybe they might think I was an undercover police officer, or someone who wished them harm or just some nut who thought he was a Bumble Bee. I felt like I needed help from a higher power and sure enough I got it.

When I had pulled into the camp I parked the van by one of the cardboard box homes that was bigger and fancier than all the rest. In was actually a series of boxes combined together that looked like more of a compound. I thought to myself, who ever lives here is someone of importance. That turned out to be oh so true. The resident of that house was The Mayor!

No, not the Mayor of Dallas–Tom Leppert who is also passionate about helping others, but the Mayor of the cardboard city. Yes they had their own mayor who ran the camp. His name was Mack. He had been homeless for many years and was well respected among the homeless. He had a quiet presence about him. I could see he was not a man to be trifled with or treated flippantly. So there I was standing by his compound. Mack came over to check me out. He didn't say a word, he just carefully looked me up and down.

I was getting nervous. Where was this all going. So I blurted out that I was the SoupMan and was there to feed the homeless. He didn't seem much impressed. Now I was getting even more nervous. I felt like I had better come up with something good before I got thrown out of there. So I looked him right in the eye and said, "may I have your permission to serve food." It was pure genius. It was pure God.

He paused a moment before answering and said, "you can feed here today," with the emphasis on 'today.' That was all I needed. At least I had my foot in the door. So that day I fed food to the homeless in Mayor Mack's cardboard city. The next day I came back again. This time I knew exactly what to do. I drove right up to Mack's compound and got out and said, "may I have your permission to serve food?" His pause was a little shorter than the day before, but his answer was the same. "You can feed here 'today.' Over the next few weeks we kept up the same dialogue every time I came. Finally one day he simply said, "you can feed here." That was it, I had Mayor Mack's blessing.

We soon became fast friends and still are to this day. Mack not only became my friend, but he also watched out for me. I heard through the homeless grapevine that he had put the word out on the street, "if you mess with the SoupMan, you are messing with me." That got my attention big time. It was good to have Mayor Mack on my side.

But it wasn't all sugar and spice out there. As I expanded the SoupMobile's operation into additional feeding locations, Mack wasn't always there to help me. I had to establish my own presence and credibility on the streets. For the most part I was able to do that. The vast majority of the homeless are good and decent people. Down on their luck yes, but decent people. However there are a few bad apples in every barrel. Early on I met one of those bad apples.

His street name was Slim. It should have been the Terminator. He was a tall, rangy, well built and in his mid twenties. He had a reputation on the streets as being a bully, but a bully who could back up his tough talk with tough treatment.

My problem with Slim started the very first day he showed up in my feeding line. My method of serving at that time was to have the homeless line up along side the van and then as they passed by I would reach into the van and hand the food to each person as they went by. Slim decided he didn't like that plan and with his long arms kept reaching past me into the van and taking food on his own. I kept telling him that he couldn't do that and he kept ignoring me. This went on for weeks.

I was getting more and more frustrated with him. Then one day I had finished feeding everyone and was getting ready to close up and head for home. Up walked Slim. I started to reach into the van to get him some food and sure enough he reached around me to get the food himself. I flat out snapped. I whirled around and looked him straight in the eye, well actually I looked **up** at him straight in the eye. He was 6'5 and I'm 5'10. Out of my mouth came these words. I said, "Slim, I want you to know that I am willing to fight you to the death to keep you out of my van."

Oh my gosh! What had I done? Did I have a death wish? Everyone else had already left. Mayor Mack was nowhere in sight. Here I was face to face with one of the meanest guys on the street. But it was too late to back down now. Now I'm not the toughest guy out there, but I can hold my own. However with Slim I knew I was out of my league. There we stood inches apart. Slim was glaring **down** at me.

I put the fiercest scowl I could on my face and just stared back **up** at him. About the only sound I could hear was the thumping of my heart. I wondered if my short career as the SoupMan was going to come to a premature end. I remember thinking, 'Oh God, please don't be on vacation today.' Well, we stared at each other for what seemed a lifetime, but I think it was actually about 30 seconds. Definitely the longest 30 seconds of my short life as the SoupMan. Things did not look good. I just kept glaring **up** at him.

Then the strangest thing happened. Slim started laughing. Yep, he burst out in loud laughter. I had no idea what this meant. Was he laughing as he was preparing to dismantle me? Was he laughing knowing that within moments I would be toast? I didn't know what it meant so I just kept on glaring. Finally he stopped laughing and looked **down** at me and said, "SoupMan, what are you, crazy. You know if we get into a fight to the death, it's gonna be your death."

I knew he was absolutely right and then I started laughing myself. So there we were, two grown men, standing inches apart and laughing loudly. So as our laugher was quieting down, I looked **up** at Slim and said, "Hey, let's make a deal. I know you are bigger than most of the guys out here and that means you need more calorie intake. So I'm willing to give you a little extra food, but how about you let me reach into the van and get it." Slim looked **down** at me and said, "OK, SoupMan, that works for me." After that I never had a problem with Slim. He was in my feeding line many times, but he never reached into the van again. In a strange way we became semi-friends.

I don't think he was used to having people challenge him. After that incident I could see he had a new found respect for me. As a bonus Slim told everyone on the street what I had done in standing up to him. That boosted my rep big time. It's important to note that guys like Slim are the exception on the streets. Yes, there are some bad guys out there, but the vast majority of homeless people are good and decent people.

Chapter 11

Dream on, Little Broomstick Cowboy

Nothing will ever be attempted if all possible objections must first be overcome.

                                      Samuel Johnson

So now the SoupMobile was off and running. We still lacked much needed money, volunteers and donors. However no worries as I just kept on flying like the humble Bumble Bee that I was. Then 15 months after the SoupMobile launch something happened that took us to a WNL—Whole Nother Level. A local Associated Press reporter (Matt) had read a small piece on us that had been published in the Dallas Morning News. Matt sent me a very cryptic email that said, "Do you believe your ministry is one of the Lord Jesus Christ?" I thought to myself, just who in the heck is this guy. He doesn't say one word about the SoupMobile or even who he was. So I sent him back an equally cryptic email saying, "Yes, do you want to help?" He quickly sent back an email saying, "yes." Those early cryptic exchanges have led to a friendship that I value deeply. Matt started volunteering with us and helped us feed the homeless.

After about five months, in November of 2004, Matt came in one day and said "I have recommended to my Associated Press editor that we do a story about the SoupMobile." I was thrilled. Here was a chance to get some publicity for our mission. Maybe his story could drum up some much need money and volunteers for us. I told Matt how glad I was he would be writing this article. He said, "no, I can't write it, I'm too close to the SoupMobile and my editor will think I am biased."

Well of course he was right. Matt was definitely biased in favor of the SoupMobile. So what Matt did was recommend a fellow AP reporter by the name of Bobby to do the story. Bobby came out and interviewed me, rode with us as we served the food, talked to the homeless people we served and put together a Thanksgiving story that ran on November 23, 2004. The title of his story was, SOUPMAN TO SERVE TURKEY ON THANKSGIVING. As part of the story he wrote that I had purchased turkey to serve the homeless out of my own pocket as a special remembrance of my late wife Peggy. The day before the story ran, I asked Bobby if he thought many newspapers would print it.

The way the Associated Press works is that its reporters write stories and those stories go out on the AP wire to newspaper editors all over the world. Each day those editors view all the stories from the Associated Press writers and print the ones they think will be most interesting to their readers. Bobby told me that since this was a Texas story, that maybe a few papers in the state would pick up the story. Beyond that he said there was no way to know. The story went out on the AP wires the evening of Nov. 22nd for editors to view and hopefully run on Nov. 23rd. I was praying for editors all over Texas to pick up the story.

Oh how limited my thinking was. Not only did Texas papers pick up the story, but papers all across the United States printed it. Our phone started ringing at 7:00AM and rang off the hook all day. People called in to both donate money and offer to volunteer. It was totally amazing. At 10:00PM that night I finally had to take the phone off the hook. All day long emails poured in from all over the country offering assistance.. By evening we had received over 1,000 emails. It was absolutely incredible. The emails were coming in so fast, I could not even keep up with reading them.

Late that night around 11:00PM something even more amazing happened. Emails started coming in from all over the world. From Germany, the Philippines, Malaysia, Japan, the Netherlands, Australia and many other countries. Editors around the world had picked up the story and printed it. I was absolutely awed by the scope of it.

Remember earlier in the book when Peggy was diagnosed with Multiple Sclerosis and I had accused God of being on vacation. Well he wasn't on vacation now. In fact it looked like he was working a double shift on behalf of the SoupMobile. We were 'Feeding His Sheep' and he was parting the Red Sea's so we could do just that. You can read the whole story Bobby wrote on our web site, www.soupmobile.org. Every time I go back and read it, a tear comes to my eyes.

Bobby's story was crucial in getting the SoupMobile the publicity we needed to get more donors and volunteers. Now you may be wondering about Matt. Bobby got all the praise and accolades for writing the story and Matt got nothing. Or so it seemed. Matt is a humble man and he told me that if God was pleased with his efforts, that's all thanks he needed. My heart was deeply touched. When we reminisce and talk about the Bobby's Thanksgiving story, Matt says "it's the best story I *never wrote*."

Chapter 12

Basketball, Anyone?

If we all did the things we are capable of, we would astound ourselves.

Thomas Edison

In the early days of the SoupMobile we were always on the lookout for funding. We are not under the umbrella of any church. We are a stand alone charity. What that means is that we are literally on our own out there in charity land. If we falter, we have no large parent organization to fall back on. What I didn't know when I started the SoupMobile was that conventional wisdom said you simply could not start a Soup Kitchen unless you were under the umbrella of a church or had a very deep pocket donor financing you. It seems I never got that memo. So not knowing we couldn't do it as a stand-alone charity, I just flapped my Bumble Bee wings and we did it anyway. Got money? If you are a deep-pockets donor who wants to Feed His Sheep, call the SoupMan.

Now I'm not knocking starting a Soup Kitchen under the umbrella of a church. In fact I regularly get emails from people around the country who have read about the SoupMobile and want to start up a Soup Kitchen in their city. They ask me for tips on how to get started. Among other things I usually advise them to get under the umbrella of a church. It's a more conventional path and you automatically tap into the churches funding and have a built in source of volunteers. So it's probably smarter to go the church umbrella way.

Of course no one ever accused me of being a conventional thinker. I just keep my focus on flapping my Bumble Bee wings. It's not too conventional, but it seems to work.

So let's get back to looking for funding in those early days of the SoupMobile. By the way, we are always looking for funding, but in the early years money was especially tight. Many times the month would start and I didn't know where the money would come from to get us through to the end of the month. So having no deep pocket donor and not being under the umbrella of a church we had to get creative.

Someone told me that the local Dallas sports arena had a deal whereby local non-profit charities could man their concession stands during their Dallas Maverick basketball games and earn a percentage of the stands profit for the night. What they required is that you brought in your own volunteer crew and took responsibility for manning the stand for the entire evening. That means you opened the stand, cooked the food, sold the food and cleaned up and closed the stand at the end of the evening. The more food you sold the more money your charity earned.

Well not having many funding sources this deal looked pretty good to me. We couldn't get rich working the concession stand, but the money we earned from it in those early days kept us afloat. So I committed us to working one full basketball season at the arena. I would be remiss if I didn't tell you how grateful I was to all the volunteers who helped me man the concession stand that season.. We had people come from all walks of life—retirees, construction workers, pastors, college students, homemakers, teachers, financial advisors, and a lot of others. You are the reason we survived financially in the early days of the SoupMobile. I will always be grateful to you all.

Even though we only worked one basketball season at the concession stand there were some issues. You see I had one small (large) problem relating to the concession stand. It seems I already had a full time job running the SoupMobile. Most days I would be up at 6:00AM to start my SoupMobile day. Then at 4:00PM on game days I would leave the SoupMobile and go over to the sports arena to work there.

Some weeks I was putting in 80 hours of work between my time at the SoupMobile and the Concession Stand. And let me tell you working the concession stand during the Dallas Mavericks basketball games was no piece of cake. Usually the arena was packed with fans and they wanted their food fast so they could get back to watching the game. Most nights we finished up and got out of the concession stand around midnight.

That year the Mavs got into the playoffs. That meant the crowds were even bigger and we were busier than ever. Working those 80 hour work weeks was catching up with me. I was running out of gas. My volunteer crew at the concession stand rotated, but as the leader I had to be there every game. I was finding out that I was the SoupMan, not SuperMan. The Mavs had reached a point in the playoffs where if they won the home game that night they would advance to the next round.

If they lost the game their season would be over and our work at the concession stand would end. I was secretly rooting for the Mavs to lose. I was exhausted. The prospect of advancing to the next round of the playoffs and having to continue to man the concession stand was not a pleasant thought. I just wanted the season to be over. So my apologies to Mark Cuban—the owner of the Mavs and to all the Dallas Mavs fans. I was rooting against you.

During the game the Mavs got way up in points in the third quarter. It looked like they were going to run away with it. That means I would be back for the next round of the playoffs and my tank was just out of gas. You might be thinking, well why didn't you just quit. NO NO NO. I had promised them we would stay for the entire basketball season. No way I was going to go back on my word. That just wasn't an option. I didn't really know if I could or even if I should approach God about this situation.

Was this the kind of thing he might get involved in? After all he might even be a Mavs fan. So I felt I could not ask God to make sure the Mavs lost the game. So standing there in the concession stand with the Mavs way up in points, I just looked up and said, "God I am totally whipped. Got any ideas." That was it, short and sweet.

Well next thing I knew the other team started chipping away at the Mavs lead. In the fourth quarter the other team caught fire and came roaring back. I was silently cheering them on. The game went right down to the wire and the other team won it on a last second basket. I remember I was standing against the concession stand wall. With my back to the wall I slowly slid down and sat right on the floor. I looked up and said, "Thank you Jesus." Sorry again to all you Dallas Mav fans. At the time I was desperate.

So did God cause the Mavs to lose the game? Well I wouldn't go that far. But this much I do know. IF the Mavs had won the game God would have found another way to bail me out. My God was not on vacation!

Chapter 13

CHRISTMAS MIRACLE

A Ship in port is safe, but that's not what ships are built for.   Grace Hopper

In August of 2005 I had an idea that at the time seemed like total lunacy. The SoupMobile was two years old. In charity land we were still just babies. A mere 24 months old. Yes, we were doing better because of Bobby's Thanksgiving story that had attracted more donors and volunteers, but we were still pinching our pennies. We had only one focus at that time and that was to feed the homeless. That task was taking up 100% of our resources. No way we could take on another project. That is no way unless you are a Bumble Bee.

My idea was to do something special for the homeless for Christmas that year. How about taking hundreds of homeless men and women right off the streets of Dallas and putting them up at a fancy hotel for Christmas. Give them all new clothes, great gifts, lots of love and a safe warm nights Christmas stay at luxury hotel. Here was a project that would test the mettle of even the largest charities, let alone the baby SoupMobile. So I floated the idea to a few of my close friends. They loved the idea and felt it would be a great project for the SoupMobile maybe five years down the road. That wasn't what I wanted to hear. This Bumble Bee didn't want to wait five years---no way. I wanted to do the project that Christmas of 2005, which was only a few short months away.

So I called a formal staff meeting in September of 2005 to discuss whether we would do the event which would come to be known as the SoupMobile's Celebrate Jesus Christmas Gala. My memories of that meeting are quite vivid. I generally laid out my ideas for the project and then went around the room asking each staff member to speak frankly and honestly about whether we should do it.

Well speak frankly they did. One by one they reminded me that we had no money for the project, no backers for the project, only three months until Christmas, no experience whatsoever running this kind of thing, a full plate with our regular feeding operation and most important, no commitment of any kind from any hotel to host the project, let alone a luxury hotel. Wow, I asked them to be frank and frank they were. As the meeting was winding down the general consensus of the staff was that they liked the idea, but it was something for five years down the road when we were more established as a charity.

So what did this Bumble Bee do? I calmly said, "great, then we will do the Christmas Gala <u>this year</u>." Jaws dropped all over the room. Looks of incredulity came over my staff members. They looked at me as if I were a lunatic. Maybe I was, but I was a determined lunatic. Determined to make the Christmas of 2005 a most magical Christmas for the homeless in the Dallas area.

However I remember there was one of my staff members that did not look at me like I was a lunatic. When I said we were going ahead with it this year, Danielle just sat there with a small wry smile on her face. She didn't say a word—she just smiled and looked over at me. Many months later I asked her what she was thinking at that time. She told me, "I was thinking there is no way we had the resources to do this project, but if anyone could pull it off, it would be you." Ah what a sweet talker she is!

So having told my staff we were GO for launch, I next decided to announce it to the world. Well the world of our charity. We immediately put out a Newsletter announcing what we were going to do. I also sent out an email to our entire mailing list telling everyone that in three short months we would be taking our homeless guests to a fancy luxury hotel and putting them up there for Christmas. I mean like hey, why just seem like a lunatic to my staff. Let's announce to the entire world that I have lost my mind. And being the Bumble Bee that I was, that's just what I did.

I felt the key to the success of the project would be getting a hotel on board. Not just any hotel, but one of the finest hotels in the world. I knew this would give our project instant credibility and be a big help in fund raising for it. On this point my thinking was correct, but there was one small problem. We didn't have a hotel on board. Think about it, what luxury hotel would let hundreds of homeless people stay there for Christmas. Even though we would be paying for it, most hotels simply would not go for it. However I figured no problem, I would just work through all my contacts in town and surely one of them would know someone who knew someone who could get us into a fancy hotel. Well, it was a great theory, but the reality was far different. A fair amount of leads came in for a hotel, but nothing was panning out. So the month of September 2005 slipped by and then October came and went. We were into November now and still no hotel. Now the pressure was on big time. I had told my known world we were going to do it and we didn't even have a hotel. Oh boy, maybe this Bumble Bee couldn't fly after all.

The next thing I knew it was Thanksgiving and still no hotel. Not even a good lead on getting a hotel. In my own head I had set Dec. 1st as the drop dead date for getting the hotel. I felt like with a luxury hotel on board, we could fund raise like crazy for the first three weeks in December and still pull it off. I was getting emails and phone calls from my supporters asking what hotel we were going to use. I told them we were still working on it.

I knew what they were thinking. They were thinking just what my staff had thought. No way this was going to happen.

So on Thanksgiving I turned to my only hope---God! We were going to find out if God was on vacation. I didn't speak to him with a lot of the's and thou's and repetitive words. I went to him just as I was.

I said to him, "Hey God, you are the one who put it on my heart to do the Christmas event this year. Have you noticed Dec. 1st is only a few days away and **I STILL DON'T HAVE A HOTEL!!!** You think you might consider parting the Red Sea for me or something???"

Yes, that was the gist of the conversation. Some people might think it's heresy to talk to God that way, but that's the way I always talk to him. I tell it straight. Yes I love and respect him big time, but I don't really think he needs a lot of the's and thou's from me. He wants me to come just as I am. So that's just what I did.

The <u>very next day</u> the phone rang at our SoupMobile office. Our secretary was out to lunch, so I answered it. It was a young man by the name of Shawn. He said he was with a local church and the church youth had make up some special treats for the homeless. He wanted to know if the SoupMobile wanted them to pass out when we went on our feeding runs. I said, "we would definitely love to have this donation." So I asked him when he could bring the treats by. He said he worked downtown during the day and could only come in the evening. Just to be polite, I asked him where he worked downtown. He said the Dallas Hyatt Regency Hotel.

A cold shiver of excitement went down my spine. I then asked him what he did at the hotel. He said he was the concierge. Another shiver! At that moment I knew God had brought me the luxury hotel I needed. At that moment I knew God was not on vacation. He was alive and well and on the job. I told Shawn about my idea for the Christmas event. He got pretty excited about it and asked how he could help. I said, "I'm glad you asked."

I told him I still didn't have a hotel on board and Christmas was less than 30 days away. He told me he thought he could help. He would go in and talk to the hotel General Manager the next day and tell him all about the project and then call me with the results.

Well the next day came and went and Shawn did not call me. And then the next day came and went. No call from Shawn. Not good. My bumble wings were flapping like crazy, but I wasn't getting off the ground. But I stuck to my guns. I had already talked to God about it and I was sure he hadn't forgotten our conversation. After all I hear he does have a pretty good memory.

Anyway on the third day Shawn did call. He apologized for taking long getting back to me, but said the General Manager hadn't been available. When Shawn had finally been able to meet with him and tell him about the project, the General Manager did not say yes or no. However he did say he was interested enough to meet with me.

Well that was all the opening I needed. I went to meet with him. His name was Dominic. When he ushered me into his office I sensed immediately that he was a man of substance and had a certain gravitas about him. This was a man that was not going to be impressed by how hard I flapped my Bumble Bee wings. He was a serious businessman, but what I didn't know at the time was that he also had a **heart of gold**. So I pitched my project to him. He had a lot of questions and he wanted answers. I didn't pull any punches. I told him the truth.

I said we were a young charity with limited resources but were determined to give the homeless of Dallas a special Christmas this year. I explained to him that I was confident that once we had a luxury hotel on board we would have instant credibility with our donors to fund raise for the project. Somehow Dominic did not look at me like I was a lunatic. As our meeting was drawing to a close he looked me in the eye and said he would approve the project. As I left the hotel my Bumble Bee wings were flapping like crazy and I was flying high. And as they say, the rest is history. We announced to everyone that the Hyatt Regency was on board and started fund raising like crazy. By Dec. 24th we had raised all the money we needed and we gave the homeless of Dallas a magical Christmas they will never forget.

After we pulled off the project that first year I started getting calls and emails from our supporters. The general theme of their communication was that they thought I was <u>nuts</u> when I announced in September 2005 that we were going to do it. One of my best supporters was a young lady named Ellen. She had been a financial donor to the SoupMobile from almost the very beginning. She emailed me and said, "SoupMan, when you said you were going to take hundreds of homeless people off the streets of Dallas and put them up at a fancy hotel for Christmas, I thought no way. No way it could be done No way you could pull if off. But you did and I salute you for it."

What Ellen didn't know at the time was that I was just a little Bumble Bee that didn't know it couldn't be done. I emailed Ellen back and thanked her for the kind note, but I corrected her in that 'I' didn't pull it off. I had a lot of help. My staff who worked overtime to make it happen, my donors who came through with the money, a hotel manager with a heart of gold and a God who seemed to like Bumble Bee's.

December 2005 was our first Christmas Gala and we ended up taking 100 homeless men and women to the hotel. In 2006 we took 200. In 2007 it was 300. In 2008 it was 400 and every year thereafter 500.

Each Christmas Gala has brought its own unique set of happenings. Let me tell you about a few of them. The 2006 event stands out because of the finances. We already had one event (2005) under our belts and we felt confident (not cocky) about pulling it off in 2006. But there was one catch. In 2005 we took 100 homeless people to the Hyatt. In 2006 we doubled that to 200. Basically that doubled the cost. Remember in 06 the SoupMobile was still barely over 3 years old. Still a baby in charity land. We were still operating on a shoestring and once again needed to fund raise like crazy.

As we approached Christmas many individuals had donated money but we were still coming up short to pay for all 200 homeless guests. So as per usual I turned to my ace in the hole. I approached God and basically said, "Hey God—SoupMan here. You know you're the one who put in on my heart to bump the number of homeless guests up to 200 this year. Christmas is just a few days away and I don't have enough money to pay for them all. I surely would appreciate it if you can send me some loot." That was it. No the's and thou's, no long winded discussions, just plain talk. I believe that there are many ways to approach God.

Some people may prefer the's and thou's and longer prayers. I'm not saying my way is the best way and certainly it's not the only way. I think the key is that God wants all of us to approach him just as we are. Nothing fake, nothing put on, just real talking. So approach him the way that works best for you.

Anyway back to my shortage of funds for my 200 homeless guests. I had my say with God and left it at that. I didn't tell anyone that we were short of funds and I didn't spend much time thinking about it. Then something amazing happened on Dec. 24, 2006 during our huge reception in the Dallas Hyatt Regency Ballroom attended by all of our homeless guests, our donors, friends and supporters.

Totally out of the blue, volunteers started coming up to me and giving me money. Checks, cash and even change. I was amazed by this because I hadn't told anyone we were short of funds. Anyway as I was putting the money in my pocket I was doing some quick math. We were getting closer to making it over the top, but we were still short. So I thanked God for the outpouring, reminded him we were still short and then thanked him 'in advance' for finding a way to put us over the top. And the way he put us over the top was totally 'off the chain.' For you city folk, that means totally amazing.

During that same reception where people just started giving me money, we had several of the local Dallas TV stations there filming the event. That evening coverage of the event was all over the evening news. A local home builder and his wife saw the news coverage. Up till then they had not known about the SoupMobile. They were so impressed by what we were doing that they wanted to help.

They tried to call the Hyatt that night to get in touch with me but the call never got through because I was literally wearing about a zillion hats running the project. So the next morning a message was waiting for me at the front desk from the local home builder to call him. I called him and thanked him for his interest and asked how I could help him. He said, "no, it's how can I help you." He asked me if we needed money for the project. I told him as a matter of fact we were still short in our fundraising. He said he could give me five.

I replied, oh five hundred, that would be great. He said, NO–NO–NO SoupMan. Not five hundred, FIVE THOUSAND. Now that's what I'm talking about! God had come through again and the home builders check put us over the top. Thanks to God, this Bumble Bee was flying high. As this book went to press I heard that my generous donor of that $5,000 had passed away. No doubt he is up in heaven right now looking down with joy on our Christmas Gala.

Another story I remember took place at the 2007 event. It was Christmas Eve night and all our homeless guests were safely in their rooms and bedded down for the night. At the '07 event we had taken 300 homeless people and we were packed to the gills. About 3:00AM that night I got a call from the front desk. They said a homeless person had just walked into the hotel lobby asking for food. They knew he wasn't one of our 300, but the front desk asked me to come down and talk with him. That 3AM call wasn't a problem, because I never get a bed the night of the 24th so I can be on constant alert if our homeless guests need any help. So I came down and introduced myself to him. His name was John. He said he was homeless and had just gotten into town that evening and he was hungry and had nowhere to stay. He asked me if I could help him. I wasn't sure what to do. We were already completely booked up and after all it was three o'clock in the morning. I considered giving him some food and sending him on his way. Somehow that didn't feel right.

So I looked at him and said, "wait right here for a few minutes and I will be right back." I left him and walked around the corner back to a secluded section of the hotel lobby. I started talking with God. I said, "I have a situation here. What should I do?" Well I will tell you flat out that I did **not** hear God talk to me in a big booming voice. In fact I didn't hear God say one word. What happened was that a powerful thought came into my head. It said, **MAKE ROOM AT THE INN.**

A cold shiver went down my spine. On my, I had always approached God and said my stuff short and sweet and here he was bringing it right back to me short and sweet. 'Make room at the inn.' Well he didn't have to tell me twice. I would have given John my bed, but remember I don't sleep the night of Dec. 24th, so I didn't have a bed. But by gosh, my NON-VACATION God was telling me to make room at the inn and make room we would. I went back and got John and said, "There's room at the inn for you tonight."

He started to softly cry and then began to thank me. I said, "Don't thank me, it was a good friend of mine who told me to make room at the inn for you." He looked at me with a blank stare and I just winked at him and said come with me. Here is how we got him a bed.

The night of the 24th we had a volunteer crew staying all night at the hotel helping us with floor duty and supervision. Those volunteers were in separate rooms so they could catch some sleep in shifts during the night. I knocked on one of those volunteer doors and a sleepy eyed young man answered the door. He saw me and said "What's up SoupMan." I told him John's story and how he needed a bed for the night.

Without hesitation he said, "no problem, I will sleep on the floor and John can have my bed." The spirit of Christmas was alive and well at 3AM in the morning and there was 'Room at the Inn.' I wonder if 2000 years ago someone would have given up their bed if they knew who was waiting outside in the womb of his mother Mary. You know who I'm talking about---HIM, the ONE, yes baby JESUS!!!

One of my favorite parts of the Christmas Gala is the very beginning. At 9:00AM on Dec. 24th, Christmas Eve Day, six huge gleaming busses pull up to the front door to the hotel loaded with all of our homeless guests. They step off the busses onto a 300ft RED CARPET. Yes, just like at the Academy Awards.

That Red Carpet is lined with thousands of volunteers who are clapping and cheering as our homeless enter the hotel. At the same time a marching band is playing the Rocky theme song. I don't know who gets more out of the Red Carpet experience, the volunteers manning it or the homeless walking it. What I do know is that it's a magical beginning to a Christmas that will not soon be forgotten.

What's most amazing about the SoupMobile's Christmas Gala are the huge number of volunteers who come out to help us with the event. It literally takes an army of volunteers, donors and supporters to make it happen. Thousands of volunteers give up parts (if not all) of their own Christmas to make sure our homeless guests have a special Christmas.

These volunteers, donors and supporters are the true heart and soul of the SoupMobile and the Christmas Gala.

So if you are reading this book, I know what you're thinking. Hey, how can I be part of the SoupMobile Celebrate Jesus Christmas Gala? Well it's simple, just go to our web site **www.soupmobile.org** and read all about it. The magic date to remember every year is November 1st. On that date our website goes live with all the Christmas details. You can go right online, look over all the available Christmas volunteer opportunities, pick the one you want and sign up right on line.

If you come and volunteer with the SoupMobile at Christmas it will be the best Christmas gift you ever **give** and it will be the best Christmas gift you ever **receive.** When you see the tears in the eyes of the homeless guests and the smiles on their faces, your heart will be touched in ways it has never been touched before. Come and join the SoupMan and his fabulous SoupTeam and share in our dream of making it a magical Christmas for the ones Jesus calls the 'least of these.'

Chapter 14

Camping Under the Stars

I believe that one of life's greatest risks is never daring to risk.

Oprah Winfrey

In the winter of 2007 I decided to do something I had never done with the homeless. On the streets of Dallas the homeless call me the SoupMan. I have been privileged to meet and come to know thousands upon thousands of homeless men and women. I have fed them, bandaged their cuts and wounds, become friends with them, laughed with them, cried with them, visited them in jail, sat with them in the large cardboard boxes they call home, watched them fail miserably, and at times watched them succeed beyond anyone's wildest dreams. Yet there was one thing I hadn't done. I had never slept overnight on the streets with the homeless.

So that winter I decided I would forgo my cushy bed and peaceful nights behind locked doors and venture out onto the hard streets of Dallas. I decided to do this for two reasons. One was to show solidarity and support for my homeless friends, and the second was to find out 'up close and personal' what it was like to sleep on the streets just like the homeless do every night. I did not tell anyone of my plans. I knew if I did they would try to talk me out of it. They would say it was too risky. But I was committed and determined to follow through. So during the winter of 2007, I slept out on the streets overnight with the homeless on two separate occasions.

The first time I carried a backpack loaded with a thin blanket, a bottled water, a sandwich and a granola bar. I carried Two Dollars in my pocket. I had made it a point not to eat any food that day. I wanted to hit the streets feeling the same hunger the homeless felt. I did not take my car, but put on my backpack and hiked to the location where I would be sleeping outside with the homeless.

That first night out on the streets was not a fun night. It wasn't like sleeping in the backyard of our house in a tent when I was a kid. This was for real. It was cold, dark and windy. I'm not embarrassed to admit that it was a little scary. There were no locked doors, no police protection, and I had to fall asleep trusting that none of the hundreds of people sleeping around me would do me wrong.

Here are some of my impressions of that night as I laid on a slab of blacktop and huddled under my thin blanket. I noticed how incredibly cold it was. It seemed like the blacktop just radiated the cold right up into my bones. Of course there was no thermostat to turn up the heat and I couldn't go into my closet to get an extra blanket. And just like the hundreds of other homeless people out there, I was on my own. I carefully hoarded the small amount of food that I brought with me. I know once it was gone, that was it. No midnight visit to the fridge and no late night trip to the 7/11 store.

One of the moments I will never forget was about midnight when I was finally able to start to drift off the sleep. In those final minutes as my breathing slowed and my eyelids started to droop, I realized I was going to be sleeping and had absolutely no protection against anyone doing me harm.

No locked doors, no police protection and no recourse if trouble started. For me those last few minutes before I fell to sleep were the most dicey moments of the entire affair. At that moment I really needed God NOT to be on vacation. Finally sleep came, and then all too suddenly I heard voices shouting. Okay, 'time to get up, get a move on.' It was 5:30AM, pitch black and some security guy was moving us off the blacktop parking lot where we had bedded down for the night. We all scurried about gathering up our things and getting ready to hit the road. No reading the morning paper, no hot breakfast, and no hot cup of coffee.

The first thing I noticed as I was gathering up my belongings was that it was still very cold and I had absolutely no way to get warm. After a night of sleeping on the blacktop my bones were stiff and my hands seemed frozen. And I was hungry. The night before I had decided to save my granola bar. Oh, was I glad I did! I greedily opened up the wrapping and carefully ate every bit of the bar, even the crumbs. I even licked the wrapper when I was finished. So with breakfast over I finished packing up. In those next few moments hundreds of homeless people started moving out in different directions and vanished into the pitch black morning that seemed as if it was still night.

As I moved out with stiff limbs and cramped cold feet, I knew where I was heading. I was hiking it back to my place. But that hike back wasn't as easy as I thought it would be. Here I was hiking through deserted dark streets with a backpack on my back and $2.00 in my pocket. I felt like a marked man. I was alone and had absolutely no one else to rely on if trouble materialized.

What if some unscrupulous guys decided I was an easy mark? What could I give them if I was stopped? My two dollars? Somehow I didn't think they would be satisfied with that. I also felt like a marked man in another way. What if the police saw me hiking through the darkened streets early in the morning with a backpack on. Would they think I was up to no good? Would they ask me what the heck I was doing out there? What would I tell them? 'Hey officer, it's okay, I'm the SoupMan and I just wanted to spend a night out with my homeless friends to show them support.'

Oh yeah, I'm sure that would have been totally believable. I mean like what kind of person *chooses* to sleep outside with the homeless? Well in this case, a Bumble Bee person!

Fortunately I made it home safely without any trouble from the bad guys or questioning by the police. So having survived that first night out sleeping with the homeless, I decided I needed to do it again just to be sure the first time out had been the real thing. A few weeks later I ventured out again and slept on that same blacktop parking lot with hundreds of homeless people. Guess what? Yes, it was almost an identical repeat of the first time. Still no fun, still dark, still cold, still hungry and I still felt like a marked man as I hiked back home in the dark the next morning.

So what did this whole experience do for me. Well it gave me an empathy for the homeless that went beyond anything I had ever know. I had already built up an incredible compassion for the homeless as I had fed and cared for them over the years. Now it went even deeper. In those two nights on the streets I got to experience firsthand what they have to go through every night. All the uncertainty, all the fear, all the hunger and the feeling of being a marked man.

It also gave me a renewed thankfulness to the Lord for what I do have. Whenever I get the urge to complain or grumble about my circumstances, I just think back to those two nights on the streets, and I quickly look upward and thank the Lord for what I do have. I am truly a blessed Bumble Bee!

Chapter 15

Myths about the Homeless

Things are not always what they seem.
—Saturday Evening Post, Feb. 19, 1876

If you have never worked with the homeless, you may have some misconceptions about them. Let's talk about a few of them. I can promise you that when it comes to the homeless things are not always what they seem to be.

One Myth is that all homeless people are lazy. I often hear the following statement from non-homeless people, "I have a job, why don't they get a job--they must be lazy." On the surface that seems to make sense. After all the vast majority of homeless people are men and most of them are able bodied and could work. So why don't they go and get jobs. Ah, well there's the rub.

Imagine if you will, two equally qualified men going to apply for the same job. One man is not homeless and the other is homeless. As they begin to fill out the employment application the non-homeless man writes in his address, his phone number and that he has transportation. The homeless man fills in his application this way. Address—I live in a cardboard box under a bridge. Phone–No phone, just call out for me as you drive by. Transportation–None. Which of these individuals do you think the employer is going to hire?

It will be the non-homeless man, and you can't really blame the employer for making that choice. It's simply good business. Added to the plight of the homeless applicant is that he doesn't have daily access to getting a shower, clean clothes or even adequate food. Most homeless people want to work. It's just very difficult for them to compete in the job market and get hired. Some of you may be asking, well just how did they become homeless in the first place. After all they weren't born homeless. In fact most homeless people at one time held down jobs, had a home or apartment and paid taxes just like any other citizen.

But for a variety of reasons they lost their job. Reasons that include jobs moving overseas, downsizing, medical problems, and drug and alcohol problems.

Which leads us to our next Myth. All homeless people are on drugs or are alcoholics. This is simply not true. Yes, some are addicted, but let's face it, drug and alcohol problems cross all strata's of our society. From the very richest to the very poorest.

They say the difference between a homeless man on drugs and a Hollywood Movie star on drugs is the Betty Ford Clinic. When the homeless guy gets caught he usually goes to jail, but when the movie star gets caught he usually goes to rehab. The difference between the two is money, but they both have the same addiction. However we tend to get down on homeless people who do drugs and we buy movie tickets for movie stars who do drugs. Seems a bit unfair doesn't it?

Another Myth that dogs the homeless is that they are bad people and up to no good. Again not true. The vast majority of homeless people are good decent people. Down on their luck yes, but good people. Are there some bad apples among the homeless? Absolutely! But then there are bad apples in any strata of society. I walk in both world's and I don't think it's any more or less among the homeless.

Here's another Myth many wonder about. What about those guys on the corners at the stop lights who have signs that say stuff like, 'Will Work for Food,' and 'Please Help.' They are homeless aren't they?

Not necessarily. In fact sometimes it's a total scam. Here's an example of how it works. A group of non-homeless men will meet up at the leaders' house early in the morning. They will all hop in the back of his pick up truck and the leader will drive these non-homeless men to different streets corners and drop them off. All the men have dressed down to look homeless and all of them are carrying signs that are designed to make you think they are homeless. All day long these men will work the corners asking drivers who get stopped at the light for money.

Then at the end of the day the leader drives his truck to each corner to pick up his crew. They all go back to his house and count up the money and divide it equally among them. It's a total scam. In fact if a homeless person tries to work one of the gang's corner, they will be driven off. So how can you know for sure if that person on the corner with the sign is really homeless. The answer is, you can't know for sure. What I recommend is that you do NOT give to those guys on the corner. Instead find a reputable charity that you know actually serves and help's the homeless and give your money to them. There are many fine charities out there who service the homeless that you could donate to. It could even be the SoupMobile–HINT, HINT!!!

Another Myth is that homeless people are just plain ungrateful for anything you give them. Well this one is patently false. Quite the contrary, the homeless we serve are extremely grateful for the food and assistance. Let me give you an example. This is a true story that took place a few years ago.

I had just finished up my daily mobile feeding run and was headed back to SoupMobile Headquarters. I spotted her on the side of the road. She looked thin and malnourished and as if she had not eaten for days. Instantly I knew she was homeless. I pulled the mobile van to the side of the road and asked her if she would like something to eat. She quietly nodded her head yes. I asked her what her name was and she said "Laura." I packed up a bag of food and handed it to her.

She carefully placed the sack on the ground and then literally threw her arms around me with a bear like hug. As I hugged her back, she wept quietly in my arms, and whispered a soft thank you in my ear. Tears flowed gently from her eyes, and if you looked real close, you might have seen a few tears falling from the SoupMan's eyes as well.

Another time I was still at my mobile feeding location, but had just finished up and was getting ready to close the van door and head back to headquarters. One of the homeless men who had been in my feeding line that day came back over to me. He graciously thanked me not only for serving him, but also for serving his fellow homeless men and women. I told him he was welcome and that we felt privileged that we could feed them. He responded, "Hey SoupMan I want to give you some money." I replied that the food was free. He said, "no, I want to help." Then he reached into the pocket of his thread bare blue jeans and pulled out all the money he had. It was NINE CENTS.

Yes, nine copper pennies. You could have knocked me over with a feather. Here was a homeless man, giving me ALL the money he had to help me feed homeless people. I thanked him profusely. To this day that nine cents is the smallest single donation I have ever received, but I promise you it's the most priceless.

It reminded me of the story in the Bible about the widow who gave two mites. It reads in Mark 12:41: And Jesus sat over against the treasury and beheld how the people cast money into the treasury---and many that were rich cast in much. And there came a certain poor widow, and she threw in two mites, which made a farthing. And he called his disciples to him, and said to them, "Truly I say to you, that this poor widow has cast more in, than all they who have cast into the treasury: for all they did cast in of their abundance; but she of her want did cast in all that she had, even all her living."

Because the SoupMobile is a non-profit charity we absolutely rely on donations to fund our operation. That nine cents didn't buy much actual food for the homeless, but it touched my heart deeply. That's one donation I will never forget. Many people give out of their abundance. He gave out of his poverty. Truly amazing! Jesus surely would have been proud.

Chapter 16

Cajun Cooking, Anyone?

Anybody can make you enjoy the first bite of a dish, but only a real chef can make you enjoy the last.

- Francois Minot

Well it doesn't take a rocket scientist to figure out that a soup kitchen needs a chef. In the early days of the SoupMobile I was the chef. Now one would think that someone who has the nickname SoupMan would be a pretty good cook. One would be wrong. I have many talents, but cooking isn't one of them. Ironic isn't it.

In the early days of the SoupMobile I had a double whammy. Not only wasn't I the greatest cook, but because we didn't have a lot of volunteers at the time I would often wear many hats. Cooking, answering the phone, sending emails, loading the mobile van, washing the dishes and whatever else needed to be done.

Many times I would have a pot of soup or stew on the stove and then I would have to run off on another duty and by the time I got back to the stove the food would be--- ah, well, let's just say slightly burned. But since there was no time to make a new batch, I would throw in some salt and pepper and seasoning to try to dissolve the burnt taste. Sometimes I was successful, but others times the homeless would notice the burnt taste. They would kid me and say, "hey SoupMan, looks liked you burned the food again today." I would just laugh and say, "no way, that's Cajun Cooking." Cajun of course being code for burnt!

So I really need a professional chef, but we couldn't afford one. So back to the source I went. Yes, God. You may have noticed by this point in the book that I often go to God for help. You know, he doesn't seem to mind. If fact I think he kinda likes I when I come and talk with him.

By the way I don't just talk with him when I need help. After my 15 year odyssey of railing against him, we have become pretty good friends. I noticed he didn't hold it against me when I called him every name in the book back then. It truly humbles me to see how incredibly forgiving he is.

Okay, back to my chef story. So here is the gist of what I said to him. "God you put it on my heart to feed the homeless. Have you noticed I'm a lousy cook. How about sending a professional chef my way." End of story. No endless pleadings, no woe is me, just this simple Bumble Bee letting the God of the universe know I needed help. About a month after my request to God, the phone rang.

I so very much appreciate the inventor of the telephone, Alexander Graham Bell. When the phone rings for me, it's usually good news about 99% of the time. When that 1% of not so good news comes, I just pretend I'm a Bumble Bee! Hey, no sense making life any more complicated than it has to be. Anyway the phone rang and it's a gentleman whose name is Gene. He said he found the SoupMobile on the internet and wanted to know if he could come and volunteer.

A lot of people find the SoupMobile on the internet. I so very much appreciate the inventor of the internet, Al Gore. Sorry Al, I just couldn't resist. I told Gene we had several volunteer opportunities at the SoupMobile and asked him if he had any preference. He said in a quiet voice, "Well I do like to cook." A cold shiver of excitement went down my spine. I notice when God is moving in my life I get a lot of cold shivers of excitement down my spine.

At that moment I knew my God was not on vacation and had brought me a chef. Chef Gene, as we affectionately call him, is an amazing man. Years ago he was a cook in the Army and served in Vietnam. He and his fellow cooks would literally fly in on helicopters into the heart of the jungle to serve food to the troops. Talk about feeding under pressure. Every day at the SoupMobile, Chef Gene is working under a deadline to get the food ready for that day. He never panics, never falters, never says it can't be done. Chef Gene finds a way to pull it all together. He's the Bumble Bee of the cooking arena. He's also a man I am proud to call friend.

After his Army days Chef Gene eventually moved his family to New Orleans where he worked for an electric company for many years. Then something happened on the morning of August 29, 2005 that would forever change the course of Gene's life. You may remember reading about a little weather event called Hurricane Katrina that hit the coast of Southeast Louisiana that fateful morning in August of 2005. Knowing the hurricane was coming Gene had already sent his family ahead to Texas for safe haven from the storm. He stayed behind to man his station at the electric company to make sure that power would be available to the citizens of Louisiana as long as possible. Believe me when I tell you, that's just the kind of guy Chef Gene is. He has a heart of gold and is constantly putting others first.

Like thousands of others, Gene's home was destroyed by the hurricane. As soon as he was able, Gene came to Dallas to reunite with his family. He had worked faithfully for his company for many years but now felt it was time to retire. He and his wife Pat decided that they would begin a new life in Texas. Gene is not the kind of guy to just sit around and watch the grass grow. He wanted to volunteer somewhere and that's when he found the SoupMobile on the internet. Thanks again to Al Gore!

Chef Gene is a GREAT cook. When he does Cajun cooking it's the real thing. Not like the SoupMan's Cajun (code for burnt) cooking. He will not let anything go out of his kitchen that he would not eat himself. His food isn't just nutritious, it's great tasting. He doesn't use many recipes, it just all comes out of his head. As for putting spices and seasoning in the food, that's an art all to itself. He puts a pinch of this, a sprinkle of that and voila, food fit for a King or Queen.

Most important Chef Gene put a special magic ingredient in every dish he prepares. You can't buy this magic ingredient in the store and you can't grow it in the field, but he uses it in abundance. That magic ingredient is LOVE. He tells his assistants at the SoupMobile, "If you don't make it with love, then we just won't make it." So for all you cooks out there, if you want to have the experience of your life, come and volunteer at the SoupMobile in Chef Gene's kitchen.

By the way, I do need to talk about Chef Gene's stove. His stove is so clean, you could take a magnifying glass and would not be able to find a speck of dirt on it. I made the mistake one time of going into Chef Gene's kitchen. He had just finished cooking the meal and had not had time yet to clean his stove. Naively I offered to clean it for him. He gave me a look like I had threatened to take away his first born child. No way was he letting anyone clean that stove, but him. I meekly slunk out of the kitchen and never made that mistake again. For me Chef Gene is just one more example of how God is not on vacation.

As it says in Roman 8:28, "And we know that God causes all things to work together for good to those who love God, to those who are called according to His purpose."

That verse says he works 'all' things together for the good. Even Hurricanes!!!

Chapter 17

The Three Amigos!

Oh Lord, please make me the person my dog thinks I am.   A Dog Owner

In the early pages of this book I told you about my late wife Peggy and her passing on her 48th birthday. When she died it was just me and Thelma, my faithful dog. We both grieved deeply over our loss. And even though Thelma is a dog, I know she experienced true sorrow when Peggy left us. For months after Peggy died, Thelma and I would bolt up out of the bed in the middle of the night if we heard even the slightest sounds that might endanger Peggy.

But of course Peggy was gone. Many times we did that and I would sadly look at Thelma and say, "she's not with us anymore." Those were some long nights for both of us. I felt so bad for Thelma that I decided to get her a companion. Another dog to be her friend and playmate. This would not be an easy task. You see Thelma was the protector of the house. She was fiercely loyal to Peggy and myself. And even though she only weighs 8lbs, she is a tiger when it comes to protecting me from any perceived threat.

Thelma is a type A dog and needs to be top dog. Bringing another dog into the house would have to be handled delicately. I thought carefully about what type of dog Thelma might accept. I felt it had to be another Chihuahua. It also had to be one that would always weigh less than Thelma and a dog that would be happy to be a side kick and not the Alpha dog. It would have to be a dog that would love to run and play and most important would bring joy to Thelma.

So what do you do when you have a wish list like that for a dog. Simple, you go to God. I said to him, "God, my Thelma is grieving and needs a companion. Please help me." I didn't figure God needed a lot of details. He already knew what was happening. So that weekend I set out in search of a Type B Chihuahua to be Thelma's playmate and companion. I heard about a local flea market that had some people selling dogs. I thought maybe this wasn't the best place to buy a dog, but it just seemed right. In I went and found a pen full of baby Chihuahua's. I picked several of them up trying to surmise which one would be the perfect companion for Thelma. None of them seemed right.

Then the dog owner said to me, try this one. She's a pure bred Chihuahua with great blood lines. I picked her up and held her by my face and she started licking my ear. I knew she was the one. Because she was pure bred, I had to pay top dollar for her. She was worth every penny. I decided to call her Louise.

I brought her home and crossed my fingers that Thelma would accept her. Well I shouldn't have been the least concerned. Thelma's qualities of loyalty and protector took over, and little Louise came under Thelma's protection, just like Peggy had. Louise turned out to be the perfect side kick. She grew to 6lbs at maturity so she is still 2lbs lighter than Thelma. She loves being the side kick and has no aspirations to be the Alpha dog. Most important she is a total joy to Thelma. Well Peggy was gone, and now it was just the three Amigos. Me, Thelma and now Louise. One final footnote on Louise. They had told me she was a pure bred dog when I purchased her.

The first time I took Louise to the vet for a checkup the vet asked me what her mix was. I said, "no mix, she's a pure bred Chihuahua." The vet chuckled and said "I'm afraid not." He said I should take her back for a refund. Then I laughed. I replied "Not a chance." No way I was going to split up the Three Amigos. Louise was perfect for Thelma and she wasn't going anywhere.

Meanwhile I continued to grieve about Peggy. For me there would not be another woman in my life. After Peggy died I decided that there would be no one that would replace her. I simply could not imagine being with someone else. I determined that the three Amigos would be my new life. I put an invisible sign on the door that said, 'No Women Allowed.'

I didn't bother to consult God on this decision. I knew beyond any doubt that he would agree with me. No need for me to even mention this subject to God. I knew what I was doing. I would be just fine with Thelma and Louise. But this was one time when God did NOT honor my wishes. He had other plans. And I am so thankful he did.

This is one of the things that make's God so totally cool. Sometimes we can goof up in our requests to him. Sometimes we don't know the right thing to do or ask of him. Sometimes we simply don't know what's best for us. He doesn't penalize us for that, but as it says in **Ephesians 3:20,"Now unto him that** is able to do exceeding abundantly above all that we ask or think, according to the power that works in us."

So what God did was basically ignore my decision of 'No Women Allowed.' Just like I had found Louise for Thelma, he would find just the right woman for me.

Chapter 18
God Sends the SoupMan His SoupGirl

I don't believe in Miracles, I depend on them.

Unknown

About six months after Peggy died and while I still had my invisible sign posted, 'No Women Allowed,' Shana showed up on my doorstep. How that happened was a **miracle** in itself. Shortly after Peggy's death, a small local homeless newspaper in Dallas called the Street Zine had called me and wanted to do a story about the SoupMan and the SoupMobile. I said yes, and the story was set to run in their January 2005 Quarterly issue. However somehow their wires got crossed and the article did not run. I didn't think much about it at the time and let the matter drop. Then a few weeks before their April quarterly issue was to run, I got a call from the paper. They had a new editor and she had noticed my story had slipped through the cracks and had not been published. She asked me if I wanted it to run in the April issue. I said, "sure, that would be just fine."

The article ran, but remember this was a very small paper with a very limited readership. I didn't know it at the time, but God was going to use that small paper to bring me my SoupGirl.

At the time I did not even know Shana was on the planet. I was busy running the SoupMobile and Shana had never even heard of the SoupMan or the SoupMobile. Here's how God remedied that situation. Shana was at a house warming party and outside on the sidewalk a homeless woman by the name of Cindy was selling issues of the April issue of the Street Zine to earn a little pocket money. Shana noticed her and asked how she was doing. Cindy said fine and asked her if she would please buy a paper from her. Shana said yes. Thank God she said yes. She then proceeded to thumb through the paper and saw the article on the SoupMan. She was intrigued and told her friends she wanted to go and volunteer at the SoupMobile to help serve food to the homeless.

A few days later I got a call at the SoupMobile. It was Shana. She said, "Are you the SoupMan guy they wrote about in the homeless newspaper." I said, "I was." She asked if she could come and volunteer. Of course I said yes. We always welcome volunteers. After all they are the heart and soul of the SoupMobile. So Shana came and started volunteering once a week. She had a real heart for helping the homeless. Everyone liked her. I looked at her as just being a good volunteer. That was the extent of my thinking. Remember I had my, 'No Women Allowed' sign posted. There was NO chance that the SoupMan would have a SoupGirl in his life. Well Shana started coming more often. I thought that this was great. Dependable volunteers are always a blessing. Then she started spending more time volunteering on the same projects I was working on. Little did I know that Shana was becoming interested in the SoupMan. In fact I was totally clueless that Shana had taken a liking to me. Typical man, huh. We are always the last to know.

One day I came to work and my secretary said to me, "you know David, Shana really likes you." I naively answered, "oh I like her too, she's a great volunteer." My secretary said, "no you don't understand, she REALLY likes you."

I said, "no way, can't be, not possible." My secretary just smiled and said, "you'll see." Well that night as I was sitting at home with Thelma and Louise on my lap, I told them what my secretary had said. Thelma and Louise didn't have much to say, but I could tell that they wanted me to stick to my 'No Women Allowed' policy. The Three Amigos were not interested in a fourth amigo.

The next time Shana came and volunteered I couldn't help but look at her in a little different light. My 'Do Not Disturb' sign was still on, but I did remember what my secretary had said to me about Shana liking me. But no matter as I was determined not to break up the Three Amigos.

But God had a different plan. In Shana he created a woman that has an amazing presence about her. I had never met anyone who had such a passion for helping her fellow man. She has a kind and loving heart and she truly believes in the words of Jesus when he said, "Feed My Sheep."

I also noticed she was pretty darned cute. A woman who is as beautiful on the outside as she is on the inside. Shana knew about Peggy's death and even though she had taken a liking to me she was totally respectful of my invisible 'No Women Allowed' sign. She kept volunteering and patiently waited for God to work things out.

Well as time went on my 'No Women Allowed' sign started to flicker on and off. It wasn't that I was playing hard to get, it was just that adding a fourth amigo was a pretty big step. However I couldn't deny that Shana's loving heart was starting to take its hold on me. So I started deliberately spending more volunteer time with her. I started looking at her differently. Not just as a volunteer, but as a possible blessing sent right from God himself. And as they say the rest is history. After a 'brief' courtship that lasted over three years we got married on October 18, 2008. Now it's the Six Amigos—Me, Shana, Thelma & Louise and my wife's two cats, Mikela & Xavier. Once again God proved to me that he is not on vacation.

As I look back on Shana's **miracle** arrival in my life, I notice that God brought this wonderful blessing to me through my life's work, which is the SoupMobile. We feed, shelter and care for the homeless year around. I believe that God honored my work and used it to bring Shana. She did not show up on my doorstep by accident. Jesus said, "Feed My Sheep." I was obeying his command and he seemed to be blessing me for doing just that.

It's my belief that when we reach out to our fellow man in love and kindness, God takes big time notice of that and blesses us even more. It's not that we give to others to get God to give to us. It doesn't work that way. We do the good deeds because that what our heart leads us to do, not to get the rewards. But God makes sure we get the rewards anyway. I can tell you from personal experience that giving to your fellow man is far more satisfying than one could ever imagine. I've lived my life both ways. Early on when it was 'all about me' and now when it's all about 'Feeding His Sheep.' I can promise you the later is far more fulfilling. When it was all about me, enough was never enough. I always wanted more. More money, more stuff, more success and more, more, more. Now when I 'Feed His Sheep' it's more, more, more about reaching out in love to my fellowman.

There's one final thing to tell you about the Shana story. Remember I told you the article about me was to run in the January 05 issue of the homeless paper? Well if it had run in that January issue as it was supposed to, Shana would have never seen it. She would have not been at the house warming party, and Cindy would not have been there to sell her the paper.

It was God who made sure that the article got delayed and ran in the April issue. That's when he knew that Shana would be at the house warming party and Cindy would be there to sell her a paper. Some would say that all of this is just coincidence. Not this Bumble Bee. It was all God!

Chapter 19

How about You???

Only a life lived for others is a life worthwhile!

Albert Einstein

Well, if you've read this far, it is my fervent prayer that you will begin your own journey of reaching out to the less fortunate in our world. Maybe for you that journey has already begun and now you want to do more.

Has the time arrived in your life to start making a real difference in the lives of the ones Jesus calls the 'least of these.' Is this the time of your life when you find a way to begin reaching out to your fellowman with love, caring and compassion.

We can't all be Mother Teresa's but in our own unique way we can make a real difference in the world. Within each one of us God has planted a seed of Love. And when that seed sprouts, that's when we start to touch lives in a powerful and passionate way.

For those of you who are already making a difference in this world, I would challenge you to 'up your game.' I would challenge you to use even more of your skills, your talents, your finances, your passion and your love to reach even greater heights as 'together' we reach out to the hurting and suffering in this world.

I would challenge you to find your passion, find your niche to help the less fortunate in this world. The key for all of us is to 'get started.' Take that first step. The Chinese Philosopher, Lao Tzu said, "The journey of a thousand miles must begin with a single step." I would urge you to take that step now.

Let me finish by thanking for for taking the time to read our story. I pray you have been blessed!

(TURN TO NEXT PAGE FOR EPILOGUE)

EPILOGUE

As they say, time marches on. This book was originally published in December of 2008. Now as we look to the future a lot has changed at the SoupMobile. Originally founded in 2003 on a wing & a lot of prayers, the SoupMobile is now in its second decade of service.

Since our blissful union in 2008 my wife Shana, a.k.a. SoupGirl and I have celebrated many absolutely glorious, dazzling, marvelous, splendid, off the chain, wondrous and groovy years of marriage. Heaven surely must be missing an Angel because she's right here with me!

Our Celebrate Jesus Christmas Gala has grown tremendously over the years. 2014 marked the 10th Anniversary of the event and many more have followed. Every Christmas we take 500 homeless men, women AND children & we now put them up at the spectacular downtown Dallas Omni Hotel. More than 2,500 volunteers come at Christmas and help with the event.

In 2009 we started a shelter program for the homeless. Our goal is to take a homeless man, women or entire family off the streets, put a safe roof over their heads, help them get jobs and eventually return them as working productive members of the community.

In 2012 we opened the SoupMobile Thrift Store.
The store trains and employ's homeless men and women and helps them prepare for a meaningful place in society. As a bonus, all the profits from the SoupMobile Thrift Store go towards our missions of 'Feeding & Sheltering' the homeless.

Even more exciting is that in honor of Christ, in 2015 the SoupMobile built a church for the homeless in Dallas, Texas. SoupMobile Church is the 'home Church' for the homeless in Dallas. A Church where they receive the call to Christ every week. At SoupMobile Church the homeless are the 'Members' and if you and I attend, we are their 'Guests.' Additionally the Church provides job training, life skills training, counseling and has lots of wholesome activities like picnics and barbecues.

Yes, the SoupMobile has seen a lot of wondrous changes since this book was first published in 2008 and our founding in 2003. However one thing hasn't changed! One thing has remained constant! One thing has remained timeless! And that one thing is Christ. In Hebrews 13:8 it says, "Jesus Christ the same yesterday, and today, and forever." Any success the SoupMobile has had is directly attributable to Christ. <u>HE</u> is the one who has continually parted the Red Sea for the SoupMobile. <u>HE</u> is the one we look to as we forge ahead into uncharted waters. HE is the one that assures us that "We can do all things thru Christ who strengthens us."

Let me finish this Epilogue with this final thought. I humbly consider myself to be the most blessed man on the planet. I have a wife who is absolutely amazing, a job that's unbelievably rewarding to my heart, a staff that is beyond compare, an army of SoupMobile friends, supporters and prayer warriors, and a Savior who made it all possible.

Thank you Jesus!

Signed, David Timothy, a.k.a. SoupMan

Email: david@soupmobile.org

Website: www.soupmobile.org

SEE NEXT PAGE FOR DETAILS ON THE SOUPMOBILE DREAM TEAM

SOUPMOBILE DREAM TEAM

No matter how you slice the cake it takes real dollars & cents to 'Feed & Shelter' the homeless. We want you to know that the SoupMobile does not receive (nor do we ask for) any City, State or Federal funding. We are a true stand-alone charity that is modeled on the early church when Jesus walked the earth. We rely on financial help from people like you to fulfill our mission.

It only costs *$5 per month* to be a member of the **SoupMobile Dream Team**. Yes, that's it—only *$5 per month*. You might think your **$5** per month isn't enough to make a difference but when added to the donations of thousands of other Dream Team members your $5 can and will make a lifesaving difference in the life of a homeless person.

At the SoupMobile we 'get it' that not everybody can write out a check for $100, $500, $1,000, 10,000 or more, but for most people $5 per month is a reasonable number. 2,000 years ago Jesus said to **'Feed My Sheep.'** Your $5 per month Dream Team membership will help us do that very thing. More details on the SoupMobile Dream Team can be found at: www.soupmobile.org